F. (Frank) Brinkley, Arthur J Mundy,
Kakuzo

Okakura

Japan : described and illustrated by the Japanese

F. (Frank) Brinkley, Arthur J Mundy,
Kakuzo

-

Okakura

Japan : described and illustrated by the Japanese

ISBN/EAN: 9783741174841

Manufactured in Europe, USA, Canada, Australia, Japa

Cover: Foto ©Andreas Hilbeck / pixelio.de

Manufactured and distributed by brebook publishing software
(www.brebook.com)

F. (Frank) Brinkley, Arthur J Mundy,
Kakuzo

Okakura

Japan : described and illustrated by the Japanese

SECTION VIII

JAPAN

OBSERVANCES AND PASTIMES.

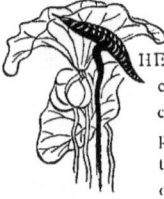

(*Concluded.*)

HE boys' *fête* (*tango*) on the fifth day of the fifth month is a particularly conspicuous event owing to the fact that at every house where a male child has been born during the preceding twelvemonth a carp, made of paper or silk, is raised, banner-wise. The carp is attached by its mouth to the end of a flag-staff, and being inflated by the breeze, undulates overhead, so that, throughout the days of this observance, thousands of big fish seem to be writhing and gyrating above the roofs of the cities. In Japanese eyes the carp typifies indomitable resolution. As it sturdily faces the stream and leaps up the waterfall, so fond parents hope that their little lads will rise in the world and overcome all obstacles. The sweet-flag and the iris, now in full bloom, play a conspicuous part in this *fête*. Bunches of the former, together with sprays of mugwort (*yomogi*) are raised at the eaves of houses, and *saké* seasoned with petals of the iris is the beverage of the season. Sprays of the sweet-flag that have thus been exposed are believed to imbibe the medicinal dew of heaven, and are consequently placed in the family baths for the invigoration of bathers. In the alcoves, warriors, battle-steeds, armor and weapons of war often beautiful and brilliant examples of skilled workmanship and decoration—are ranged, but these relics of bygone days are fast losing their interest for the youth of the nation, and since it is impossible to combine picturesqueness with accuracy in any representation of the military uniforms and accoutrements of modern times, alcoves that used once to be crowded with gallant puppets in gorgeous panoply now make no contribution to the gayety of the *tango*. Tradition tells us nothing certain about the origin of this celebration. Some of its details—as, for example, the fact that the rice cakes peculiar to the time are wrapped in bamboo leaves and the bean-confections in oak leaves, or that, at the hour of the hare, all lights are extinguished for a brief interval in temples and houses—have their own special legends to explain them, but the festival as a whole is a mystery. We cannot pause here to enter into minutiæ, neither have we space to speak at any length of the series of flower-*fêtes* that mark the various seasons, the picnics to the wistaria, the azalea, the iris, the lotus, the peonies, the chrysanthemums, the orchids and the autumnal tints. The ideal of the Japanese is to have a festival of flower or foliage for every month, but their manner of enjoying themselves on these occasions is uniformly simple. They do not carry with them stores of provisions and hampers of wine, but are content with the fare that the local tea-house offers, and to have indited a felicitous couplet and suspended it from the branch of some notable tree or from the stem of some luxuriantly blooming plant, is to have attained the summit of enjoyment. Were it possible to banish the spasm-shouts that men mistake for songs and the twanging of the unmusical *samisen*, the out-doors *fêtes* of Japan would be the acme of refined pleasure-seeking.

OUT-OF-DOOR MUSIC AT NARA.

We pass by the ceremonies of the sixth month when at twilight by river-banks *Shinto* priests set up cross-shaped periapts (*gohei*) and pray for the dispersal of evil influences, or, into the stream thus purified, cast miniature paper surcoats, shaped by the hands of worshippers and bearing the legend, " Peace be on this household " (*kanai anzen*). The growth of modern ideas tends to weaken the people's fidelity to these purely religious rites, which, indeed, might well be spared from the nation's customs. Very brief reference will also suffice in the case of the *sekku*, on the seventh of the seventh month, for few persons now place faith in the cakes (*sakuhei*) which, eaten upon that day, were formerly supposed to avert ague; nor is the " marriage of the stars " regarded any longer with even traditional curiosity. Yet the latter legend once inspired a pretty ceremony. Four tables used to be placed in the garden—especially in the park of the " Palace of Pure Freshness," for the custom was always favored by the Imperial family—and thereon, flanked by smoking sticks of incense, vessels of water were set, to reflect the passage of the heavenly river (*ama-no-kawa, i. e.,* the Milky Way) by the Herdboy Prince (*Tanabata*) on his way to meet the Weaver Princess (*Ori-hime*). Connected with this ceremonial—purely Chinese in its origin—was the writing of verselets upon thin sheets of bamboo or fine-grained woods, and these *tanzaku*, as they are called, ultimately took the form of dainty tablets, decorated with devices in golden and silvern lacquer and tasselled with silk cords, many of which have found a place in Western collections merely for the sake of their prettiness. To this seventh month, however,— it must not be forgotten that we adhere to the terms of the old calendar, and that the so-called seventh month corresponds, approximately, with August, to this seventh month belongs a celebration which retains much of its old vigor, and can never be entirely neglected so long as ancestral worship is the national cult. It is a *fête* known as *Urabon*, or more commonly *Bon*, intended for the welcome and entertainment of the spirits of the dead which are supposed to visit their loved survivors at this season. The nature of the occasion will at once suggest the profound sentiment connected with its observance. Five days are devoted to the rites, though it is not to be supposed that these are of an elaborate or complicated character. The chief duty is to prepare the *shoryodana*, or spirit-altar. It is a small mat of straw, having at the four corners bamboo pillars, between which is suspended the inevitable "sweet-air rope" (*shime-nawa*) with pendent decoration of wave-shaped vermicelli, sprays of chestnut, dried persimmons, yew berries, ears of millet, white egg-fruits, gourds and winter cherries. Over the straw floor are strewn bull-rushes and leaves of the cockscomb and lespedeza; within the enclosure stand rods thrust into melons or egg-fruits which are cut into shapes of oxen or horses,—spirit vehicles,—and around the whole is erected a low belt of cedar leaves. The details are inviolable. Viands are, of course, provided for the use of the ghostly visitors. There are the cakes of welcome (*omukae-dango*) and the cakes of farewell (*okuri-dango*); there are rice-balls wrapped in lotus leaves; there is a humble dish called *imo-no-zuki*, which consists of potato-stems boiled and seasoned with soy, and there are fruits varying in kind and quantity according to the means of the household. Lanterns

SHUZENJI VILLAGE, PROVINCE OF IDZU.

This village is very popular on account of its mineral waters. A hot spring rises between the rocks in the very middle of the river.

are suspended before each house, and at eventide on the 13th, tiny fires of hemp are lit to greet the coming spirits, and a vessel of water is placed outside that they may wash their feet. Again, on the night of the 16th, these feebly flickering lights shed their rays on the path of the departing visitors, and so the *fête* ends. The preparations are elaborate; the rites and observances, of the simplest. It might be supposed that since the aerial visitors are regarded as guardians and assistants of their kinsfolk on earth, this, their one annual visit, would be converted into an occasion for propitiating their favor and enlisting their aid. But hospitality does not suggest that a guest should be importuned with petitions. There is some sprinkling of powdered incense over the embers of the hempen bonfire in order that the fumes, mingling with the ghostly essences that permeate the air, may smother evil influences; sometimes, too, men light their pipes in the flame, thinking thus to inhale good fortune; sometimes they step over the fire to avert or heal certain maladies, and sometimes they preserve the cinders as a charm against disease. But the spirits come and go unworried by petitions. Neither their advent nor their presence inspires feelings of awe or horror. The average Japanese is not without a dread of ghosts, and may easily be persuaded into a quiet but firm conviction in the reality of a haunted house, but the spirits that come to visit him in his home at *Bon* time are friends whom he loves and trusts. His disposition is to receive them with dance and song rather than with shrinking and aversion, and it thus fell out that among the multitude of Japanese *fêtes*, none was so conspicuously marked by dancing performances. We speak in the past, for these *Bon* dances have fallen under the ban of the law in modern Japan, and though still practised in the provinces, are no longer to be seen in the great cities. It is on record that, some two thousand years ago, men and women of all classes, princes and princesses of the blood not excepted, were wont to assemble upon hill-tops or in the streets, and to engage in dances one object of which was identical with the motive of the modern ball, namely, to promote the interests of love. This custom was subsequently modified -- like so many other Japanese customs --by Chinese influences, but much of its ancient character was certainly preserved in the *Bon* dances which the civilization of new Japan taboos.

It is probable that very few foreigners ever learn to appreciate Japanese dancing. One reason for their want of sympathy is that they approach the study with prejudiced minds. Their conception of dancing is that it must be either musical gymnastics deriving their charm from harmony of sound and motion, and pleasurable chiefly to the performer, or a spectacular display, like the Occidental *ballet*, representing large combinations of graceful movements, enhanced by splendid scenery and accessories of painting and sculpture. But in Japan dancing has primarily a mimetic purpose. With rare exceptions, the dance represents some historical incident, some mythical legend, some scene from the realm of folk-lore or superstition. The technique is elaborate, and although the motions never suggest muscular effort or display abnormal contortions, it is nevertheless certain that physical training of the most rigorous character cannot be dispensed with, and that the very ease of the seemingly smooth and spontaneous action results from art hidden by its own perfection. It is also certain that the mechanics of the dance are as nothing to the Japanese spectator compared with the music of its motion, and that he interprets the *staccato* and *legato* of its passages with discrimination amounting almost to instinct and, in some degree, hereditary. In exceptional cases the foreigner's perception may be similarly subtle, but he must generally lack the faculty of apprehending the esoterics of the dance, and thus finds himself in the position of a man at an opera who has no *libretto*, or a play-goer without a knowledge of the plot. We have already seen that from prehistoric times dancing constituted a prominent feature in the worship of the deities, and that it had its origin in the fable which represents the inhabitants of heaven dancing before the cave into which the goddess of the sun had retired. From the sphere of religion it appears to have passed quickly and widely into the every-day life of the people, until at last the practice acquired a vogue unparalleled in any other country. Volumes might be written descriptive of the numerous dances taught to girls from their tender years, and, on a much smaller but still extensive scale, to boys also; and as for the repertoire of the professional expert, it is virtually inexhaustible. There have been occa-

GEISHAS OF THE YOUNGER CLASS.

sions when the whole of the inhabitants of a city turned out in costume to celebrate some noted event by a universal dance. By such means did the citizens of Kyoto exhibit their joy when the capital of the empire was transferred to their city from Nara at the end of the eighth century, and by such means also they evinced their gratitude for a year of prosperity in subsequent eras. The latter dance, known as *hōnen-odori*, probably stands at the head of all performances of the kind in so far as concerns the number of those taking part in it and the variety of their costumes. Each district of the city had its distinguishing color; light green silk for the East, in imitation of the dragon presiding in that quarter; crimson crêpe for the South, in unison with the plumage of the scarlet bird that soared there; black velvet for the North, to typify the dark panoply of military power; and white crêpe for the West, where the gray tiger dwelt. (These conceptions are all of Chinese origin.) These, it must be understood, were the ground colors of the dancer's garments: to the hues of the embroidered or woven decoration no limit was set, nor yet to the designs--a nightingale perched on a spray of blossoming plum; silver trout gleaming in blue streams; snowy herons roosting among pine boughs at Gion shrine; fiery maples glowing on the Kwacho hillside; rosy cherry petals floating over the Otowa waterfall, or the vulgar Venus (*Otafuku*) embracing a mushroom on Inari mountain—such and many other fancies the admirable skill of the weaver and the embroiderer depicted on the robes of this motley concourse, whose units, each disguised according to his or her fancy, as chair-bearers, as sorcerers, as pilgrims, as sailors, as grooms, as pedlers, as nurses, as dumpling-hucksters, as publicans, as apprentices, as anything and everything that did not ape aristocracy or trespass upon the domain of the patrician, danced, for hour after hour, in a maze of graceful or grotesque movement, to the music of drum and flute. Many words might be squandered on attempts to describe these dances, so delightful to Japanese senses, but the impression conveyed must be at best a mere shadow of the reality. Sometimes the performers are tiny maidens, only seven or eight years old; sometimes men of fifty or upwards are alone qualified. The *tanabata* dance on the 7th day of the seventh month, to celebrate the union of the Herdboy Prince and Weaver Princess is an example of the former. Each little lassie is dressed in strict conformity with a traditional model—a lofty coiffure, gay with pins of silver and tortoise shell; a damask kerchief jauntily knotted on the forehead; long sleeves tied into shoulder puffs with white satin cords; a richly decorated satin robe with crimson under-garment; a broad belt, embroidered and embossed with designs in gold and purple; a miniature drum, gilt and silk-stringed, with lacquered drumstick in the hands, and purple socks on the feet. Nurses, scarcely less picturesquely attired, and carrying bright-hued umbrellas with crane and tortoise patterns, accompany the little girls and take a subordinate part in the dance, during which the children sing a simple refrain in unison, and beat out the rhythm of their movements on their toy drums. The *gebon-odori*

TONOSAWA IN THE HAKONE DISTRICT NEAR YUMOTO.
Every shop-window in this village is filled with mosaic wood-work, the product of native talent.

of Wakayama prefecture is a type of elders' dancing. Seventy or eighty merchants join in the performance. They put on hats adorned with artificial flowers; wear black surcoats over white body garments; carry gourds, umbrellas, gongs and drums, and recite a religious formula as they dance. Many provincial centres have dances peculiar to the locality, the motives of the performances showing endless variety, and the costumes being of the most fanciful character. We cannot attempt to describe these. They must be seen to be appreciated. We may add, however, that the songs chanted during the dances are innumerable. Generally the ideas are trivial, and the verselets owe their value to the cadence of their five-syllabled and seven-syllabled lines---a kind of metre scarcely capable of being musically reproduced in English words--- and to the recurrence of similar sounds in different senses, rather than to the beauty or loftiness of the sentiments they embody. We append here three specimens, the first two translated from the repertoire of the *Bon* dances, the third from that of the "Flower Dance" of Bingo province:

I.

Bon, Bon, with us yet,
To-day and to-morrow pass;
Bon, Bon, ere three suns set,
Dies like the dead grass,
Dead on the winter hill,
But Bon now is with us still.

With dead grass the altar wreathe;
Overhead the red sun burns,
To peonies the dead grass turns.
Gazed at from beneath.

With dead grass the altar crown,
Silver-soft the moonlight gleams,
Flowers of ruth the dead grass seems
To spirits looking down.

Flowers of the peony
Bloom to pass away;
Bloom of the pity flower
Bides here but to-day.

II.

If you go, beloved best,
Take me with you too;
(*Nou noko sai sai.*)[1]
To the east, to the west,
If only with you.
(*Yotte kono.*)[1]

Smile or frown, joy or care,
Snow or sunny weather,

Anywhere, everywhere,
Only together.
(*Suku noka choi choi.*)

III.

If you want to meet me, love,
Only we twain,
Come to the gate, love,
Sunshine or rain;
Stand in the shadow, love,
And if people pry,
Say that you came, love,
To watch who went by.[2]

If you want to meet me, love,
Only we two,
Come to the tea-grove, love,
Moonlight and dew;
Stand among the bushes, love,
And if passers see,
Say that you came, love,
To gather leaves of tea.

If you want to meet me, love,
Only you and I,
Come to the pine tree, love,
Clouds or clear sky;
Stand among the spikelets, love,
And if folks ask why,
Say that you came, love,
To catch a butterfly.

The subject of dancing cannot be dismissed without reference to the classical mime of Japan, the *shin-gaku* of early eras, the *no* of mediæval and modern times. The *shin-gaku*, or sacred mime, represented in fragmentary form the dance of the deities before the cave of the sun goddess, and was included among the religious rites of the *Shinto* cult. A popular parody of this rite made its appearance in the seventh century and received the name of *san-gaku* or *saru-gaku*, the former a logically conceived term signifying "unorthodox mime," the latter obtained by cutting the ideograph *shin* (deity) into two and taking the right half only, which remnant was the character for the zodiacal monkey (*saru*). It is curious that the subtle sarcasm of the latter process and the slur thus cast upon the *Shinto* observance by its vulgarization should have synchronized with the government's resolve to patronize Buddhism. Japanese history draws no inference from these coincidences, but Japanese history never analyzes. The sacred dance having been thus degraded to the antics employed by a

[1] Meaningless interjections thrown in by the musicians. [2] An allusion to a method of divining.

jester for emphasizing his wit, and the light heart of the people responding readily to the innovation, there grew up the bucolic dances (*den-gaku*), briefly described above, which partook of
the nature of supplications or thanksgivings to the deities in connection with agricultural
pursuits. Buddhist priests now began to interest themselves in a custom which could not be
ignored without impairing the popularity of their creed, and whenever Buddhism laid its
hand upon anything Japanese, Chinese influences were imparted by the touch. During the
Muromachi and Kamakura epochs, that is to say, during the years when military feudalism
overshadowed the throne in Kyoto itself, and the days when it had a separate stronghold at
Kamakura, the histrionic art in China reached a high stage of development. The seven passions, of which philosophy forbade all exhibition in every-day life, found an appropriate field
for display on the stage of the theatre, and pictures from mythical, historical and biographi-
cal galleries were presented to popular gaze in a fine setting of spectacular accessories. The
Buddhist priests translated the spirit of this entertainment to Japan, and having purged it of
its purely theatrical features, grafted it on the bucolic dance, which thus sprang into aristocratic favor and was gradually enriched with a repertoire of songs embodying Buddhist
precepts as well as poetical fancies. By degrees, however, its *Shinto* rival, the *saru-gaku*,
began to raise its head, and in the middle of the fourteenth century an open-air performance
at one of the bridges in Kyoto on the occasion of an Imperial progress restored the ancient
dance to official patronage. A notable innovation had, in fact, been introduced: masks were
worn by the dancers, and the potentialities of the change were so clearly appreciated that
soon no less than sixty-six varieties of masks received the cachet of experts, and the dance
rapidly became fashionable among aristocrats, who, without the disguise of the mask, would
have hesitated to take part in such a pastime. There were of course persons who devoted
their lives to studying the art; a title (*ta-in*) was conferred upon experts of special skill, and
by degrees, under the encouragement of court patronage and the refining influence of Buddhism, which ultimately invaded this sphere also, as it had already invaded that of the
den-gaku, a great variety of mimetic dances was evolved. There is a lengthy and intricate
history connected with the evolution of these *no* dances as they were generically called, but
were it set forth here readers would emerge from the study with only a vague impression of
bewildering nomenclature. Some interest, however, attaches to the fact that as early as the
fifteenth century a special kind of *no* (*kanjin-no*, or the mercy-promoting *no*) became the pro-
totype of the charity concert of modern Europe and America. The immediate object was to
collect funds for the great Buddhist festival of Gion in Kyoto,— described in a previous
chapter,- and among the audience that honored the performance were representatives of
all the aristocratic classes, from princes of the blood to men at arms. This idea found such
favor that from having been originally a prelude to a *fête*, the *no* itself became a *fête*, and in
the prosperous days of the Tokugawa Regency a monthly performance of *kanjin-no* took
place in Yedo. Two large stages were set up, one in the west of the city (at *Shiba guchi*), the

THE NIKKO ROAD.

An ancient avenue twenty miles in length, leading from Utsunomiya to Nikko, either side being lined the entire distance by lofty cryptomerias.

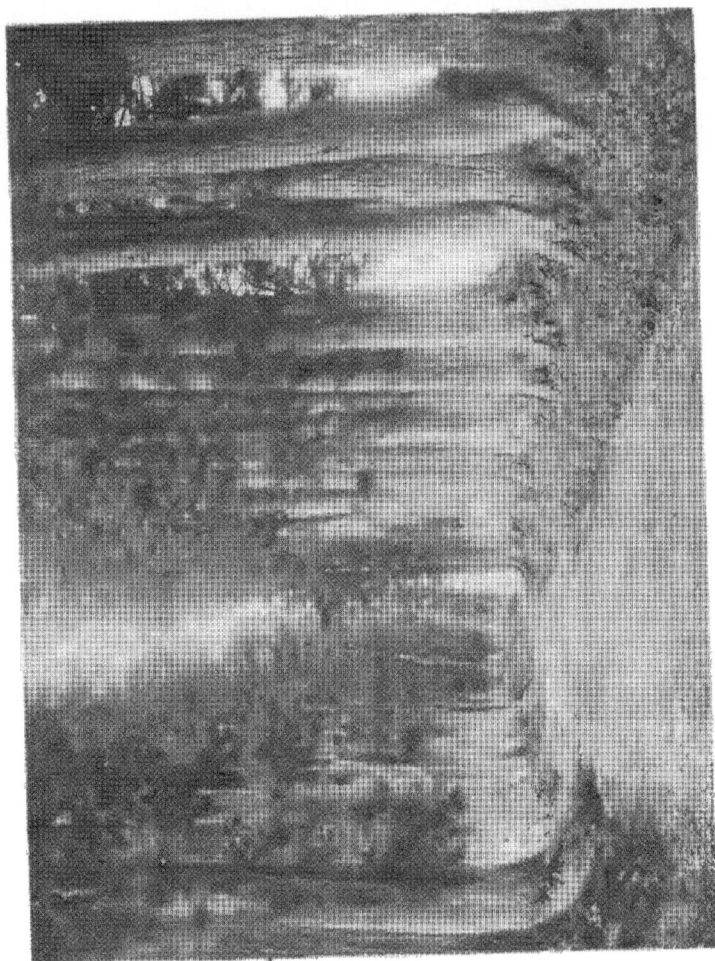

other in the east (at *Asakusa*), and upon the nobles residing in the military capital devolved the duty of providing dancers and accessories; a sufficiently onerous duty, seeing that the performance of the *kanjin-no* when at the zenith of its popularity lasted for fifteen days, that the costumes were of the most magnificent and expensive character, and that the display was expected to be on a scale sufficiently grand to compensate for the absence of all other sources of public entertainment, these being officially interdicted while the *no* was on the stage. To one variety of the dance (called *issei-ichidai kanjin-no*, or "one-life-one-generation") such honor attached that once only in a generation might it be presented to the public, and history

PRIVATE RESIDENCE ON THE BLUFF AT YOKOHAMA.

shows that during two hundred years the citizens of Yedo had but eight opportunities of witnessing this greatest of mimetic spectacles. Much might also be written about the *no-kyogen*, which, though in reality a species of comic dance intended to occupy the interlude of the *no* proper, has now come to be erroneously regarded — especially by foreigners — as the general type of the *no*; about the *sensuke-no*, which takes its name from a courageous innovator who ventured to degrade the dance by placing it upon the boards of the theatre, then (1830) an institution utterly tabooed by the aristocracy; about the *teruha-kyogen*, a modification due to the light fancy of a lady who fitted the fashionable songs of her era (1845) to the elaborate pantomime of the *no*; about the temporary decadence of the *no* at the fall of feudalism and about its vigorous revival in recent times. But such topics belong to a monograph rather than to the cursory notice for which alone we can find space here. The *no* is perhaps the most essentially Japanese thing in Japan. It has been likened to the old Greek drama because of the respect, not prescribed but instinctive, paid to the three unities, the assistance of a chorus, the stately demeanor of the masked actors, the open-air amphitheatre and the semi-religious element pervading the performance. The likeness, though certainly traceable, is purely accidental. Japanese taste has alone presided over the development of the *no*, and the power with which the spectacle of this peculiarly refined and classical drama appeals to the art instinct of the Japanese may be appreciated from the fact that they will sit from morning to evening watching with rapt attention performances which for all the splendor of the actors' costumes, the intensity of some of the situations and the combined grace and force of the motions, soon become inexpressibly tedious to the foreign spectator.

Any allusion to Japanese dancing immediately recalls to the memory of foreigners familiar with Japan the image of a girl exquisitely refined in all her ways; her costume a *chef-d'œuvre* of decorative art; her looks demure, yet arch; her manners restful and self-contained, yet sunny and winsome; her movements gentle and unobtrusive, but musically graceful; her conversation a piquant mixture of feminine inconsequence and sparkling repartee; her repertoire of light accomplishments inexhaustible; her subjective modesty a model, and her objective complacency unmeasured. Such is the *geisha*, written about, sung about and raved about by travellers whom this novel combination of fair sweetness and sordid frailty has moved to a rapture of bewildered admiration, and by "old residents" whose senses, however *blasé*, however racially intolerant, never become impervious to her abstract attractions. She is generally spoken of as a *danseuse*, but dancing, though it figures largely in her training, and though her skill in it doubtless contributes much to her graces of movement, constitutes only a minor part of her professional *rôle*. She has, in fact, no counterpart outside Japan: for while she is a mistress of all seductive arts, seduction is not necessarily her trade; and whereas she never forgets to be a lady, she takes care never to be mistaken for one. Originally—and in her case we cannot go back further than the year 1681—she was simply a dancing child (*odori-ko*), whose trade was to perform in great folks' mansions on festive occasions, and who never degraded herself by accepting an invitation to restaurants or tea-houses. But by and by (1689) the law recognized her as a demoralizing influence in military society, and feudal nobles were forbidden to make her a feature at their feasts. Thus, relegated to the places of public resort which she had hitherto eschewed, she lost caste and character, nor was it until the close of the eighteenth century that she again obtained admittance to aristocratic dwellings. In notifications issued thereafter from time to time we can easily trace the vain efforts of officialdom to limit the range of her charms. The keeping of *odori-ko* now (1800) became a trade. Instead of living with her parents or guardians, a girl, still in her tender youth, was intrusted to a *geisha-ya* (*geisha* house), and there, with three or four companions, received training in all the accomplishments necessary to the successful practice of her profession. There, also, she lived for a fixed term of years somewhat after the manner of an apprentice, her family being paid at the outset a sum of money (*minoshiro-kin*) which greatly resembled a purchase price, and her earnings after she had made her *début* being divided in exceedingly unequal proportions between her employer and herself. From ten to twenty *yen* was—and is—the amount of compensation given to parents in consideration of their binding their child to a *geisha-ya* for a period of from seven to ten years, but that outlay represents only a fraction of the expenses subsequently incurred by the employer in training the girl and providing rich costumes for her use. From the age of about ten or eleven she begins to do duty as an *o-shaku*, or cup-bearer, and at sixteen or seventeen she becomes what is technically called *ippon*, a term literally meaning "one stick." The reference here is to the fact that the *geisha's* honorarium is euphemistically measured, not by the flight of vulgar hours, but by the burning of fragrant incense. For the time occupied in burning one stick of incense she receives twenty-five *sen*, whereas the *o-shaku* receives only one half of that amount. The fact is twenty-five *sen* an hour, but the fashion of the incense fiction is scrupulously observed. It is chiefly during the "cup-bearer" period of her career that the *geisha* dances. When she reaches the *ippon* stage she makes music for her little successors of the *o-shaku* rank; plays accompaniments for the songs of the convives; sings to them herself; becomes their *vis-à-vis* in the game of *ken* or *nanko* or some other pastime; laughs merrily at their slenderest joke, and caps it with some bright conceit of her own; dances, if required, with a certain display of pretty protest; carries in and out the lacquered trays of edibles, and throws over the whole entertainment a glamour of grace, sunshine and maiden mystery, without the least *soupçon* of indelicacy so far as her own initiative is concerned. It must be plainly recorded, indeed, that in purely Japanese circles the *geisha* is essentially a refining influence, and that if she errs and leads others into error— as she undoubtedly does — her trespasses are carefully concealed from public gaze. Her twenty-five *sen* an hour is not pay or wage or consideration or any other common kind of earning: it is the "honorable congratula-

tion" (*o-shugi*). She receives in addition an "honorable flower" (*o-hana*), which varies according to the mood of her employer, but is never less than a *yen*. A statistician might infer from these figures that five hours of "congratulation" plus a "flower" — or, say, a hundred and ten gold cents—represents an excellent daily average.

THE GREAT BRONZE BELL AT NARA.

But when a *geisha* is in vogue she has invitations to "present her face" at many reunions on the same day, and even half an hour's act of presence entitles her to "one stick of incense" and one "flower." Thus she earns hundreds, not tens, of *yen* monthly. Then there is the gold that she picks up on the by-ways of her profession. She may tread them lawfully by purchasing a special license in addition to her *geisha* ticket, or she may follow them in secrecy and danger. Let it be enough to say that she exploits this mine of wealth to its extreme capacity, but without ever overstepping the limits of feminine reserve. She plays all the time for her own hand. Her quest is a lover sufficiently devoted to remove her from a professional career into private life. If she has been but a pale little star on the public horizon, this process of "redemption" is cheap. But if she has become a luminary, the compensation demanded by her employer for the loss of her services is often very large.

In this context we naturally arrive at a problem which our pledge to our readers compels us to discuss, and which, indeed, deserves some comment, if only for the sake of correcting the very false impressions that have been created by imperfectly informed critics. It has been shown in a previous chapter that the sale of human beings found a place among the transactions of Japanese trade from very ancient times, and that, though the dimensions of the practice varied at different epochs, prohibitive legislation never succeeded in stamping it out. From that source the ranks of the "priestesses of humanity" were chiefly recruited. We need not pause here to analyze the causes which chiefly contributed to the growth of the social evil in Japan. It may be supposed that, the family being regarded by the Confucian system of ethics as the very pivot of the State, a powerful motive must have operated to preserve the domestic circle against the incursions of irregular passion. It may also be supposed that, since the military structure of Japanese society did not adapt itself to permanent marital obligations, ephemeral agents of indulgence must have been in large demand. Both hypotheses are correct in a measure, but it would be wrong to infer either that an instinctive desire to maintain the purity of family life imparted moral sanction to extra-matrimonial irregularities, or that the *samurai's* prudent and often necessary abstention from marriage ties created exceptional facilities for less embarrassing relations. As to the former point, we shall probably be nearer the truth if we say that, essentially as the Japanese character differs from the usually defined Oriental type, it certainly includes an element of resignation which has no affinity with the stubborn resistance offered in the Occident even to ills that are recognized as inevitable. The Japanese long ago perceived that the natural force of certain appetites far exceeds the requirements of human well being or happiness, and instead of setting themselves to redress this hopelessly disturbed equilibrium, they preferred to accept the fact and to subject its consequences to official control. It is unnecessary to seek more recondite causes for the growth and licensing of the social evil in Japan. Neither have we to discuss the great question whether to endue virtue with vicarious respect by the uncompromising and inefficient stigmatization of vice, atones adequately for a consequent failure to check the ravages of the most terrible physical scourge that afflicts mankind. That is a problem inviting world-wide solution. The Japanese view of it is the view of continental Europe: they license prostitution. They proceed, also, a step farther than continental Europe, for they banish all the priestesses and paraphernalia of the vice to remote quarters of their cities, and enforce this ostracism with such successful rigor that the remaining quarters are absolutely free from any evidence of the evil. It has often been urged by the advocates of the non-licensing system that the ban which drives into obscurity every manifestation of the sensual passions is specially potent to diminish their indulgence. The Japanese licensing system certainly achieves that end so far as the vast bulk of the population is concerned. On the other hand, within the prescribed quarters no attempt is made to limit the resources of temptation. The unfortunate women, tricked out in rich costumes and splendid coiffures, sit ranged on a kind of proscenium, separated from the street by a widely latticed partition through which passers-by can gaze without obstruction. It is this feature of the system that chiefly shocks the foreign observer. Exceptional moral obtuseness is suggested by its crude practicality, and it seems to inflict harsh degradation on the woman for the sake of catering to the convenience and, perhaps, appealing to the imagination of the libertine. Arraigned upon that charge, the Japanese reply first, that when a man's depraved impulses have led him as far as these remote haunts of vice, little deference need be paid to his small remnants of virtue ; secondly, that by granting licenses the law constructively recognizes the holders' right to ply their trade in whatever manner appears most convenient within the prescribed limits ; and, thirdly, that to soften the hardships of the courtesan's lot may be a suggestion of mercy, but certainly is not an obligation of morality. We state the Japanese case without attempting to pass judgment on its merits. But no one can ignore that the sentence of absolute ostracism and banishment pronounced against the courtesan in Japan, so long as she pursues her evil trade, ought to have a strongly deterrent effect. She is irrevocably exiled, not merely from the society of virtuous people, but even from the vicinity of their habitations and from the places where they congregate for business or for pleasure. She lives in a species of convict settlement, scarcely ever emerging from the precincts of her prison during her term of service, and never suffered for a moment to forget the degradation into which she has sold herself. Her manner of adopting a career of shame constitutes an additional dissuasion. It is always a matter of sale. In consideration of a certain sum paid to her family, she pledges herself to serve as a *yu-jo* (*fille de joie*) for a fixed term of years. Such transactions seem to differ little from slave traffic. They appear to perpetuate the old customs referred to in a previous chapter. The law, however, actively endeavors to avert their worst abuses.[1] It is enacted that a girl must have attained the full age of sixteen before her consent can be accounted legal ; that she and her parents or guardians must attend at the office of the *police de mœurs* and signify their united desire to enter

[1] The Government of the Restoration (1867) distinguished itself by drastic legislation against transactions that pledged women to a life of shame. It issued a law dissolving, without reserve, all existing covenants of that nature and annulling any monetary obligations connected with them. It proclaimed that all capital invested in immoral enterprises should be treated as stolen, and that, since prostitutes and *geisha* had dehumanized themselves, moneys due by them, or by others on their account, could not be recovered ; and it prescribed severe penalties for any attempt to bind a girl to degrading service. But that passion of reform was soon cooled by contact with conditions that have proved too strong for legislation in all ages, and the statesmen of Japan, finding they could not eradicate the evil, adopted the wiser course of regulating it.

into the proposed agreement; that the circumstances of the career she is choosing must then and there be fully explained to her, after which a week's interval must be allowed for her to reconsider her purpose; and that the service she undertakes must be recognized as absolutely terminable by her own free choice at any moment. This last and most important condition is generally overlooked by foreign critics. They imagine that the law sanctions an arrangement by which a girl of tender years is consigned irrevocably to a life of shame and misery, whereas the truth is that the payer of the *mundium* acquires no right enforceable in opposition to the girl's volition, and cannot recover possession of her person if she quits his service. But though the law withholds all recognition of the principle of coercion, there can be no doubt that, for practical purposes, the girl is coerced. The obligation that dictated her original sacrifice remains valid until the completion of the service for which she has contracted. To abandon that service prematurely means that her family become liable for the money they received from her employer at the outset. Another obstacle usually stands between the *yu-jo* and the recovery of her freedom. Things are so managed that she can scarcely avoid contracting debts on account of her wardrobe, and these debts often compel her to accept a fresh term of degradation. Even in such a career ranks and distinctions are contrived, to rouse ambition and encourage extravagance, so that, once entangled in the meshes of shame, escape is cruelly difficult. It has been alleged by slanderers of Japanese ethics that to have been a *geisha* or a *yu-jo* is not a disqualifying prelude to respectable marriage. There is no truth in the statement. The delirium of passion is responsible for offences against social canons in Japan as in Europe, and during the period of general levelling and confusion that immediately succeeded the fall of feudalism, traditions and conventionalities were sometimes neglected. But, for the rest, the antecedents of a wife are, and have always been, scrutinized just as closely in this section of the Far East as in any Western country. The most unsightly feature of the whole system is the part played by parents and guardians in consigning their daughters or relatives to such a life. Where the promptings of filial duty possess almost the force of law, recourse to them may well take the character of coercion. There is no doubt that the Japanese daughter's estimate of her individual rights weighs little against her sense of family obligations, and that, on the other hand, her parents take a greatly exaggerated view of the obedience she owes them. Disciples of Western civilization cannot choose but condemn such ethics in the most unequivocal terms. It should be distinctly understood, however, that only the pressure of dire necessity is held to justify the sacrifice of a girl's person. The act is counted a misery by those who have recourse to it, and evokes the profound pity of friends and relatives. There are no purely voluntary victims. No one adopts the career if any possible alternative offers, and that fact must be placed to the credit either of the system itself or of the morality of Japanese women. One of the aspirations of modern Japanese reformers used to be the abolition of licensed prostitution. But it never appeared that they had studied the subject by the light of ethical philosophy, and the public declined to take them seriously.

Reverting to our story of the year's *fêtes*, we find ourselves in the eighth month of the old calendar, approximately the ninth of the new. This is essentially the dead season. In the times of the Tokugawa *Shoguns*, Yedo was required to hold a grand festival in commemoration of the fact that Ieyasu, the great founder of the Shogunate, made his official entry into the city on the first of the eighth month.

But the Tokyo of to-day eschews all acknowledgment of the fact that it was once the capital of the *Shoguns*, and in September pays homage to the moon day only. There is a Japanese saying that in spring the moonbeams lose themselves among the blossoms; in summer their image reflected from the water is more beautiful than the original; in winter they have an air of desolation; only in autumn is their charm perfect and unmixed. Hence on the 15th of the eighth month, and the 13th of the ninth, parties are formed to admire the moon; verses are composed in her praise, and in each house a table is set, bearing offerings of *saké*, rice dumplings, potatoes, chestnuts, persimmons and pears. This custom, however, like so many of the people's traditional habits, is gradually falling into disuse. In the great cities, Tokyo, Osaka and Kyoto, it has lost much of its romantic and poetic character, but its vogue is likely to be preserved by

DANCING GIRLS.

climatic and commercial influences. The delightful freshness of early autumn nights renders the moon *fête* a welcome excuse to the heat-weary citizens for an evening on the water, and owners of river-side restaurants and pleasure boats contribute industriously to the people's love of these Venetian entertainments. The water of Kyoto, celebrated for its purity and bleaching properties, comes to the city in little rivulets, and the so-called Kamo River is but a paltry stream trickling seaward over a wide bed of gravel-banks and bowlders. But the make-believe faculty with which the Japanese are richly endowed, invests this arid area with all the properties of a broad-bosomed river, and the people sup there under the moonlight as contentedly as though cool currents were rippling around them, and the breath of cataracts fanning their faces. Osaka citizens, happier in the possession of the Yodo River, which, taking its way direct from the great lake of Biwa, sweeps generously but gently through their streets, spend much of their summer-evening life floating on the water amid the flashing of fireworks and the twanging of *samisens*. But though, owing to the much greater size of the Sumida River, and the configuration of the streets, these water picnics are less in evidence in Tokyo than in Osaka, they are in reality more affected. The citizen's ideal of summer pleasure is to hire a *yane-bune*,[1] engage two or three *geisha*, and travel lazily up stream with scull or sail, debarking at one of the many famous restaurants that line both banks of the river, whence he drifts home after dinner along the path of the moonbeams, merry, musical and perhaps love-sick. These delights culminate at a *fête* called the " river opening " (*kawa-biraki*), which takes place nominally on " moon night " in August. Those for whom the *fête* is organized contribute nothing to the preparations. All that part of the affair is undertaken by the river-side restaurants and boathouse keepers, who, for the sake of the throng of customers that the celebration brings, put up a considerable sum to purchase fireworks. It is an excellent speculation. The river in the vicinity of the Ryogoku bridge, the central point of Bohemian Tokyo, is usually thronged with boats from bank to bank, and every water-side chamber has its party of guests, who pay ample prices for scanty accommodation. It is easy to conceive what a feature the *geisha* constitutes on these occasions — a girl with all the daintiest graces of person and costume; all the gentle refinements of virtuous womanhood; all the accomplishments of expert training, and all the attractions of vague morality. She is a Japanese invention and a Japanese specialty.

In autumn the chrysanthemum becomes the centre of attraction. The Japanese were once able to claim the premiership of the world as cultivators of this flower, but their pride of place has been usurped by Western horticulturists. Still the chrysanthemum, their imperial flower, the Emperor's crest and the nucleus of hundreds of exquisite decorative designs, is far more to them than to any European people. They delight in its quaintly named varieties, — the " jewel of the inner court," the " autumn amulet," the " ten-fingered-ten-eyed flower," the " snow of the pear bloom," the " sleep of the hoary tiger," the " moon-touched blossom," the " crystal palace," the " five-lake hoarfrost," the " three-treasure petal " and so on. They delight in the wonder of the blossom's dishevelled symmetry so characteristic of the equipoise and irregularity of their own decorative art. They delight in the wealth of bloom that careful nursing can produce, — as many as from thirteen hundred to sixteen hundred flowers on a single plant, — and they delight in the ingenuity of public gardeners who mould masses of blossoms and greenery into historical and mythological tableaux which even the country bumpkin and the city *gamin* are not too ignorant to appreciate. It appears that a banquet in honor of the chrysanthemum used to be one of the regular observances at the Imperial Court in ancient times, and that, at a later era, when the Tokugawa ruled in Yedo (Tokyo), the ladies of the palace there were accustomed to engage in a species of competition, each procur-

[1] A boat of which the middle part is covered by a roof (*yane*) under which the pleasure-seekers sit. The space between the pillars that support the roof may be either closed with sliding windows of paper and glass, or left completely open.

ing a chrysanthemum blossom, the choicest of which was selected for presentation to the *Shogun's* consort, rich rewards and great *éclat* accruing, of course, to the owner of the "victor flower." All these old fashions have now been merged in a garden party of Occidental type. At one of the Emperor's detached palaces in Tokyo numerous chrysanthemum plants of the finest and rarest kinds are cultivated, and during three days in October the park is thrown open to the aristocratic and official classes, the Emperor and Empress themselves appearing among their guests on the first day,— a great occasion for "globe-trotters," who, by the good offices of their country's representative, can generally procure an invitation. The resident foreigner is seldom so fortunate, unless he be in the service of the government or the recipient of a high-class Japanese decoration, but to be a stranger is to have a warrant of welcome.

Common to all seasons and essentially Japanese in their origin as well as in their developments, are performances held nightly at a species of public hall called *yose-seki*, or, in every-day parlance, *yose*. The most respectable of these entertainments is the *kōdan*, or historical narrative, known until recent years under the name of *gundan* (war story). In old-time Japan the life of the aristocrat and his doings lay entirely beyond the close scrutiny of every one outside the military class, that is to say, entirely beyond the scrutiny of fully nine-tenths of the nation. The warlike motives and methods of the patrician remained always a mystery to the commoner. Such a state of affairs would certainly have resulted

in the growth of a large school of historical romancists had the pen enjoyed any freedom. But the exclusiveness of the *samurai* asserted itself as sharply in the domain of literature as in that of society, and although records of military incidents were compiled from time to time, they never rose above skeleton narratives without a breath of animation to stir

SHINTO PRIESTS SOLICITING ALMS.

their dry bones. To Buddhist priests is due the initiative in a movement which ultimately became a useful means of familiarizing the masses with the salient events of their country's history. The priests, however, had no such purpose at the outset. The new *rôle* that they struck out, in the early years of the fourteenth century, aimed solely at opening to Japanese

aristocrats the pages of China's warlike annals. Alike in literature and in the art of war the
Buddhist friars of mediæval Japan were the repositories of knowledge, the great majority
of the *samurai* knowing only how to fight. Thus there occurred to a learned abbot (Genkei)
the idea of critically expounding the military classics of the Middle Kingdom to patrician
audiences at the Imperial Court, and the innovation attracted wide favor and patronage.

More than two hundred and fifty years elapsed, however, before a popular character
was given to these lectures. A *samurai* (Goto Matabei Mototsugu), who had himself figured
conspicuously in the warlike pageant of his time but had fallen into a state of poverty, took
his stand one day within the enclosure of the Temma Tenjin temple in Kyoto at a time of
festival, and, as a bread-earning resource, entertained the worshippers with vivid accounts of
the scenes in which he had borne a part. He quickly found an enthusiastic audience, as
well as numerous imitators among the *ronin*, or soldiers of fortune, who, not owing alle-
giance to any feudal chief, and being without a fixed source of income, were glad to turn their
hands to any profitable pursuit that did not involve a connection with vulgar trade. Gradually, by steps which we need not trace, these *raconteurs* (*koshaku-shi*) became a recognized
class ; established halls (*yose*) for delivering their narratives or readings ; divided themselves
into various schools distinguished by special oratorical methods ; devoted their whole lives
to the cultivation of their art, and developed a style to which the possession of very high
merits must be conceded. Nothing could be simpler than the method of these experts.
Seated on the mats before a species of lecturn and armed with a fan and a small flat baton
of paper, the *koshaku-shi* carries his audience with him through scenes where all the passions
that sway humanity are portrayed with admirable force and fidelity. Petty adjuncts as the
fan and the paper baton seem, the uses that they serve are extensive. A hesitating poise of
the half-opened fan introduces the audience at once to some mood of coyness or expectancy ;
a graceful sweep of its full-spread surface invokes the presence of summer airs, moonlight
dancers or stately ladies ; the sharp snap of its suddenly folded ribs suggests fateful resolve
or exhausted patience ; now its crescent rises slowly in unison with the growth of some
sound of menace or the march of some disaster's prelude ; now it sinks as hope dies or the
power of resistance fades from some hero's arm in mortal peril ; and when the tale begins
to climb to a crisis, the baton beats out a swift sharp note of warning on the wooden lecturn,
its startled raps growing quicker as incident crowds upon incident, until the rush and rattle
of the armed combat, the din and confusion of the *mêlée*, the crash of the catastrophe, seem
to be actually reproduced before the eyes of the audience.

The *koshaku-shi* uses no book. The stories that he has to tell are not fully recorded
in any public document, nor can absolute historical accuracy be claimed for them. The
figures that move through the drama and the cardinal incidents are historical; all the environment is in accurate consonance with the customs of the epoch ; but the skill of the *raconteur* or of his predecessors— for these tales are handed down as family heirlooms— adds

WRITING A LETTER.

Japanese calligraphy is artistic and beautiful. In writing with the finely pointed brush the motion is from the shoulder and not the wrist. In comparison with it, the freest, boldest European hand is stiff and cramped. The characters used are Chinese ideographs, each word having a separate sign. Letters are written on a scroll of paper, the characters standing in columns reading from right to left.

a large margin of the picturesque, the sensational and the imaginary. Yet there can be no doubt about the service these men render in familiarizing the masses with the characters and events of the national history, as well as with the social, administrative and military canons of bygone ages. The magnitude of the educational work they accomplish may be inferred when we say that in Tokyo alone they number over three hundred, divided into twelve schools, each tracing its origin to some celebrated expert, the originator of a special style, and that their repertoire of subjects includes eight sections — accounts of commotions raised by treacherous clansmen in feudal families; accounts of momentous local inter-

ACTORS IN THE ANCIENT DANCE KAGURA.
Theatrical performance before a temple to entertain the g d.

ferences by the central administration; accounts of vendettas; accounts of famous judicial decisions; biographies of renowned heroes; lives of redressers of popular wrongs; journalistic records, and critical *résumés* of contemporary events.[1]

A rival or colleague of the *koshaku-shi* is the "talker" (*hanashi-ka*), or "fugitive-words-man" (*rakugo-ka*), who differs from the *raconteur* only in the lighter character of the subjects he chooses and in the prominence that he gives to the humorous side of his performance. The founder of this school (Anrakuan Shakuden, originally called Hirabayashi Heidayu) does not belong to a very remote era (1600 A. D.) and is remembered now chiefly for the sake of eight volumes of wit and humor, the first of their kind, compiled by him at the age of seventy. Society had opened its arms to him as a master of the curious dilettanteism known as *cha-no-yu* (the tea clubs' cult) before it recognized him as a humorist, but in the end the most stately circles of aristocrats resigned themselves to laugh with him, and with a scarcely less celebrated contemporary whose extemporized songs suggested or supplemented the wit of the master. Succeeding generations did not neglect these models. Not

[1] The remuneration earned by the *koshaku-shi* is small. There are three classes, distinguished by degrees of skill. A third-class expert receives one *rin* per head of audience. Hence two hundred hearers, a good "house," means 20 *sen* (10 cents gold). A first-class performer is entitled to ten times that amount. Thus his attendance at a *yose* generally brings him a dollar (gold). He may give a *koshaku* at two or even three *yose* daily, and he is often invited to social reunions, when his guerdon varies from a dollar and a half to four or even five dollars. But there are not more than ten masters in all Japan whose reputation secures lucrative private patronage.

merely an exceptional fund of humor and large powers of mimicry, but also considerable erudition were needed for the successful pursuit of the *rakugo-ka's* career, and though it formerly ranked below that of the *koshaku-shi*, the differentiation is scarcely perceptible in modern times. Often its votaries are broken-down gentlemen whose excesses have exhausted their fortunes, but much oftener they are men of no mean literary capacity who can weave the events of their time into narratives where tragedy and comedy play equally artistic parts. For the rest, what has been written above about the *koshaku-shi's* earnings and his performance applies equally to the *rakugo-ka*. But the latter takes his subjects from the realm of romance or every-day life and does not seek to inspire his audience with any higher sentiments than sympathy and merriment. It would be difficult to decide whether he or the *koshaku-shi* is the greater artist. Both are certainly great, and each is without parallel in any other country.[1]

To speak of a *yose* as a "hall" is to suggest a somewhat exaggerated idea of its quality and arrangements. A ruder or more comfortless place could scarcely be conceived — the building rough and totally undecorated, the floor covered with mats but not divided into compartments, the gallery equally without redeeming feature except a semblance of privacy, the dais for the performers slightly elevated but entirely without ornamentation or scenic background. Such is the *yose*. A visitor, whatever his degree, pays an entrance fee varying from 2½ to 6 *sen*, makes a further disbursement of half a *sen* for the hire of a cushion, and thus equipped seats himself wherever he can find floor-space. If the weather be cold he spends a *sen* and a half on a brazier to be laid beside his cushion, and it still remains possible to squander the same sum on a pot of tea and a tiny drinking-cup, though economical folks find tea at one *sen* sufficiently palatable. Thus a total outlay of 9½ *sen* may be compassed, the return for which is from three to four hours' entertainment. The *raconteur* and the humorist are not the only performers. There are also experts in recitative (*jōruri*)[2], in juggling, in puppet playing and sometimes in dancing or music. The *jōruri* is a dramatic solo, chanted and recited with accompaniment of *samisen*. Modulation of the voice is skilfully made to suit changes of character, but for the rest no histrionic or mimetic effects are attempted. Female experts often acquire fame in this line. Being required, however, to simulate masculine tones, their performance sounds harsh and unnatural to foreign ears. The *jōruri* has its educational uses: it constructs its libretto from the tragedies of national and feudal history and familiarizes the people with names and events that would otherwise lie entirely beyond the range of their reading or traditions. In Kyoto and Osaka its heroes and heroines are frequently represented by puppets, finely modelled and tricked out in panoply of

[1] The *rakugo-ka* uses a fan only at his performance. He is not provided with the paper baton (*hari*) of the *koshaku-shi*. This trifling difference is nevertheless characteristic.

[2] "Jōruri" is the name of a lady of the twelfth century whose very sad love adventures were recorded in a species of twelve-act dramatic tale. A modification of this kind of performance, partly singing, partly recitative and always accompanied by the *samisen*, is called *gidayu*, a name without significance for Western readers.

camp or costume of court, all details strictly faithful to the fashions of the era. But Tokyo has never excelled in the manufacture of movable puppets. Its plastic specialty lies in the modelling of clay figures, galleries of which grouped to represent historical celebrities at crises of their careers may always be seen in the *sen*-shows at Asakusa under the shadow of the temple of the goddess of mercy, "the wax-works of Asakusa" as Anglo-Saxons are wont to call them.

In Tokyo alone there are a hundred and eighty *yose*. The law gives itself little concern about them, except to interdict any displays injurious to public morals and to post a supervising constable in each hall. They accommodate a total of about forty thousand people, and if each had a full audience the aggregate expenditure on account of entrance fees, cushion hire, brazier borrowing and tea-drinking would be some twelve hundred American dollars a night. So cheaply do the citizens of the Japanese capital take their pleasure.

Far older than any of the arts practised at the *yose* is the sport of wrestling (*sumo-tori*). It is supposed to date from the first century before the Christian era, and since not even the advent of Western civilization in modern times has interrupted its career of popularity, the Japanese are accustomed to speak of it as an institution nineteen centuries old. But tradition is here more fond than faithful. That a wrestling bout of historical fame took place during the reign of the Emperor Suijin (24 B. C.) is probably as credible as any event referred to the semi-fabulous eras preceding the advent of ideographs. The story says that the custom of those days was to organize a palace-guard from soldiers of eminent thews, and that among the officers of the guard one Kehaya (or Kuehaya) showed himself invincibly muscular and overbearingly arrogant. The Emperor, hoping to find a match for this trucu-

AN ORCHESTRA FOR GEISHA DANCING.

lent swaggerer, ordered a levy of the strongest men in the realm, among whom came a certain Sukune. He challenged the bully, overthrew him, trampled him to death, and received for reward a wide estate at Tajima in Yamato province. Tradition dates the science of wrestling from that event, and gives to Sukune the credit of reducing its methods to an elaborate code.

But it is impossible to sift fact from fable in this narrative. What we know for certain is that not until the year 726 A. D., when Shomu reigned, did the Imperial Court extend its patronage to wrestling, and that whatever developments the science had received before that time, its etiquette, the forty-eight varieties of orthodox grip, the gradation of its professors, the discipline of their training and the rules of their career, were gradually elaborated during and after the eighth century. Shiga Seirin of Omi was the master expert in the days of the Emperor Shomu, and for four hundred and fifty years the duties of chief umpire (*gyoji*) were discharged at court by successive generations of his descendants, until the line became extinct in 1187 A. D., when Yoshida Iyetsugu of Echizen succeeded to the post, receiving from his sovereign the name of Oikaze, with high official rank. Yoshida Oikaze's house is still flourishing, and to its representative alone belongs the right of bestowing the highest

INTERIOR OF ASAKUSA TEMPLE, TOKYO.

One of the most popular temples in Japan. It is a great holiday resort. Altars and toy-shops jog elbows.
The enclosure is filled with small stores of all kinds, together with miniature theatres.

distinction that a wrestler can obtain, a cable-cincture (*yokozuna*) twisted out of two thick strands of white silk. It is not easy, nor would it be interesting, to trace the processes by which wrestling passed from the primitive programme in which one champion pitted himself successively against all comers, to the present elaborate system of camps and ranks. Like the dramatic dances described above, the sport served almost exclusively for aristocratic entertainment, until, in the last quarter of the seventeenth century, the Tokugawa Government permitted charity performances (*kanjin-zumo*) to be held in Yedo (Tokyo), the proceeds being devoted to the repair or construction of temples and shrines. Further, like all exercises of dexterity or ingenuity, wrestling received a great impetus during the last two centuries of feudalism, when each fief had its own champions, and interfeudal rivalry supplied a keen incentive to effort of every kind. It is said that in those palmy days of patronage, wrestlers attained a stature of seven feet and a weight of over four hundred pounds. Such men are no longer seen, though in height and bulk the modern wrestler offers an extraordinary contrast to his average fellow countryman: the latter measures sixty-two inches and weighs a hundred and fifty pounds; the former, in the first five grades, has a height of seventy-two inches and weighs two hundred and fifty pounds.[1] This striking difference has led many foreign observers to conjecture that the wrestler belongs to a special race. Such is not the case. The ranks of the wrestlers are recruited chiefly from the farming, fishing and woodman classes. In early youth a lusty lad is apprenticed to some master of the art, and after long years of severe training and strict diet, he makes his *début* in the ring. His food is coarse but wholesome. In quantity it is supposed to be double that of an ordinary man. Nothing is interdicted save alcoholic excess. All the wrestlers in the empire are now divided into two camps, the eastern and the western, and the occupants of the camps are subdivided into classes. Each camp has its three champions, called, in order, the "great seat" (*o-seki*), the "seat-divider"—*i. e.*, middle-seat—(*seki-wake*), and the "front-head" (*mae-gashira*). Next come those "within the curtain" (*maku-no-uchi*) and those "below the curtain" (*maku-no-shita*), and then follow six classes down to the novice (*mae-zumo*). There are usually from twelve to thirteen "within the curtain" in each camp, and from thirty to fifty "below the curtain." The numbers in the other classes vary largely. Twice a year, in spring and in autumn, within the enclosure of the *Eko-in* in Tokyo, twice also in Osaka and Kyoto, and once in each important provincial centre, grand matches are held between the two camps; champion against champion, curtainer against curtainer, and so on. The combats take place in a sand-strewn ring, 24 feet in diameter, surrounded by a low rim of straw sand-bags. Planted immediately outside the rim, four posts mark the seats of as many "elders," and

[1] The average height of the adult male Japanese, according to Dr. E. Baelz, the best authority on the ethnography of Japan, is 5 ft. 2½ inches, and that of the adult female, 4 ft. 8½ inches. Thus the male in Japan is about as tall as the female in Europe. The weight of the male is 125 lbs. in the lower orders, and from 115 to 120 lbs. in the upper (against an average weight of 150 to 160 lbs. in Europe); the woman weighs from 102 to 105 lbs. It will be convenient to set down here some salient facts as to the physical structure and properties of the people, following always the authority of Dr. Baelz. The Japanese grows only 8 per cent of his stature from the time of puberty, whereas the European grows 13 per cent. The bulk of the people are strong. The upper classes are comparatively weakly, but the lower are robust and muscular. In the matter of weight, as well as in that of height and to a still more notable extent, development ceases sooner in the Japanese than in the European. The head is large, the face and torso are long, the legs short. Indeed, the length of the torso and the shortness of the legs are so marked as to constitute a valuable race characteristic. In a European the length of the leg from the trochanter to the ground is more than one half of the length of the body; in the Japanese it is distinctly less. The face, in consequence of the low bridge of the nose, is less prominent than that of the European, and appears to be broader, but is not really so. The forehead is low; the vertical distance between the tip of the nose and the upper lip, very small. The mouth is sometimes small and shapely, but frequently it is large and the teeth are prognathous. The eye is always dark, generally of a fine brown. It seems to be oblique, but the obliquity is due to the position of the lids. Further, the upper lid is almost a direct continuation of the skin of the forehead, instead of being recessed under the eyebrow, as is the case in Europeans. The cheeks are broad and flat; the chin narrow; the legs are often crooked and graceless, especially in women; the calves are strongly developed; the ankles thick; the feet broad; the arms, hands and neck remarkably graceful; the skin is light yellow, often not darker than that of southern Europeans, but sometimes as dusky as that of the Singhalese. The Japanese belong to the least hirsute of the human species. Their hair is black and straight. It turns gray at the age of 45 to 50, but baldness is comparatively rare. Dr. Baelz concludes that the finer type of the Japanese came from the borders of the Euphrates and Tigris, and finds a resemblance between them and the Egyptians.

within the circle stands the umpire, dressed in the ceremonial costume of old times, and carrying a silk-tasselled fan, his badge of office. The contestants, wearing only loin-cloths and fringed girdles, enter the ring from their respective sides, salute the audience, spread their hands to signify implicit obedience to the umpire's rulings, strew salt in token of amity, stretch their muscles, stamp their feet, and finally face each other, sitting on their hams, in the centre of the circle. At this stage the umpire's responsibility is great. He has to see that when the men spring into grips—a consummation often preceded by many challenging attitudes on one side and refusals on the other —both are at the same stage of inhalation or

A WRESTLING MATCH.

The wrestler is a distinct type of man and may be detected almost at a glance. The shape of the head and the manner of dressing the hair are prominent characteristics. The umpire is a person of great importance and is usually a retired wrestler.

exhalation, and neither obtains an advantage unrecognized by the subtle rules of the science. The commonest grip is an interlacing of the arms, or a grasp of the opponent's girdle, and victory depends on throwing the adversary or thrusting him out of the ring,—one foot outside the sand-bags suffices. The most skilled champions are like fine fencers: they exert their force within narrow limits, their attack is delivered at short range, and their movements, though powerful, are always under strict command. Except to the initiated such play looks comparatively tame; the dash and spring, the fierce fight for grips and the headlong struggle of the novice are far more animated and picturesque. Imperturbable good humor presides at all these contests, and a struggle is never permitted to outlast the scientific application of strength. If the umpire sees that both combatants are hesitating from exhaustion, he separates them, and, after a brief interval, replaces them in their former grips. Sometimes he separates them altogether and declares the combat a draw. The excitement of the audience occasionally rises to fever heat. Men throw their garments to the victor, and redeem them afterwards by money payments. Ten days is the duration of a bout, and the emoluments of the wrestlers vary from one yen to fifty, independently of presents received from the audience. These men are not in the least degraded by their rough profession. They are honest, simple, kindly fellows, never degenerating into bullies or drunken law-breakers. Such an incident as the arrest and punishment of a wrestler is virtually unknown. The goal of the career is to become an "elder" (*toshi-yori-yaku*), which fortune falls to the lot of those who have distinguished themselves by specially meritorious service in the cause of their profession. There are now some eighty elders. They organize the matches, administer the finances, act as referees, and take pupils. This last privilege does not belong even to a champion. Wrestlers who see no hope of becoming so distinguished as to secure special patronage, or of gaining admittance to the elders' rank, quietly retire to their native province and live by manual labor. There has been nothing in their professional life to unfit them for resuming the habits of their rural ancestors.

Out of the mimetic dances so popular in Japan it may be supposed that the histrionic art would have grown at an early era, and that its development would have been rapid. Facts do not indorse such an inference. The drama proper was, indeed, born of the mimetic dance, but its nativity was curiously belated, and that it was born at all seems to have been, in great part, the result of accident. Many writers have been content to dismiss the subject with the curt remark that the Japanese theatre is of Chinese origin, and that the passage of the institution from one country to the other must be classed among the fortuitous incidents of neighborly intercourse. But there are obstacles to the acceptance of that superficial view. In the days when the Ashikaga Shogunate was at the zenith of its power, the theatre had not yet made its appearance in Japan despite the long and, at times, intimate intercourse that had existed with China. The mimetic dances, of which we have already spoken under the general name of *no*, were, however, in wide vogue, and elaborate arrangements for their performance on occasions of festivals existed in several of the great temples. They served, in short, not merely as an aristocratic pastime, but also as a means of replenishing

STEPS AND GATE LEADING TO THE TEMPLE INSIDE THE MAIN ENTRANCE AT SIBRA PARK, TOKYO.

the coffers of the shrines. A little later than the middle of the sixteenth century, the national shrine of Izumo was found to be in need of costly repairs, and one of its vestals (*miko*), O-Kuni, an exceptionally skilled dancer, whose posturing in the *kagura* (sacred dance) at times of worship had become famous, undertook to visit Kyoto for the purpose of enlisting assistance. She danced before the *Shogun* Yoshiteru, and pleased him so much that he issued orders for the repair of the shrine. There the story might have ended and the evolution of the Japanese drama might have been indefinitely postponed had not a very old-fashioned element come upon the scene. Among the retainers of the *Shogun* was one Nagoya Sanzaemon, whose duties consisted in superintending the arrangements for court festivities. Sanzaemon and O-Kuni fell in love with one another, their liaison was discovered, and they were dismissed from the *Shogun's* service. The woman's wit suggested that they should earn a livelihood by practising in public the accomplishments they had acquired at the shrine and in the *Shogun's* court, and thus they took to dancing on the sward of a common which may be seen to-day by any one visiting Kyoto and making his way to Kitano Shiba-wara (the Kitano moor). The name given to the scene of their performance and still used in the sense of " theatre "— *shibai*, or the sward (*shiba*) seat (*i*)[1]— perpetuates its rustic beginnings. O-Kuni's dance before the *Shogun* had been the immemorial *Ama-no-iwa-to*, the mythological deities inviting the sun goddess to emerge from her cave. What modifications she introduced for popular purposes it is impossible now to determine. The main fact is that she and her husband converted the mimetic dance from a religious rite or an aristocratic pastime into a bread-earning profession, and thus laid the foundation of the theatre. History is accurate enough to tell us something about O-Kuni's favorite costume — a wide-brimmed lacquer hat, a red rain-coat, a string of beads about her neck, and also that she often took the *rôle* of a man, assigning the female part to her husband, while one Densuke acted as buffoon. They had an immense success and found many imitators, but always among the lowest elements of the population. The Kyoto *filles de joie* seem to have thought this kind of enterprise[2] especially suited to their station and capacities. At the initiative of the still remembered Sadoshima Masakichi, they erected a stage in the dry bed of the river, and thus received the name " river-bed folk " (*kawara-mono*), an epithet significant of the contempt in which their profession was held. Sadoshima and her troupe, now including a number of performers of both sexes, made their way to Yedo (Tokyo) at the beginning of the seventeenth century. But if they had any hope of improving their status by this change of location, events disappointed them. Within the crowded precincts of the " eastern capital " not even a river-bed offered space for their purpose, and they were obliged to betake themselves to the degraded quarter — a suburb which had just sprung up on a site previously overgrown with reeds,

[1] The origin of the term is interesting. When the Imperial Court was at Nara (eighth century), pestilential vapors were found to proceed from a cave near one of the temples. The dance of *Okina Sanbaso*, to which allusion has been made in speaking of New-Year observances, was danced on the sward before the cave to dispel the evil influence, and people spoke of the performance as *shibai*, in allusion to the place where it was held.

[2] It was called *kabuki*, of which the ideographic significance is a performance (*ki*) of song (*ka*) and dance (*bu*). As to the origin of the word, however, some allege that it was a corruption of *katamuki*, to sway or overturn, and that it was used with reference to the transports of delight into which the audience ought to be thrown by such displays of skill. However that may be, the point to be noted is that the popular form of mime was named *kabuki*, as distinguished from the aristocratic *nō*. To this day one of the principal theatres in Tokyo is called *Kabuki-za*, and the term might be properly applied to any place employed for histrionic representations.

the notorious *Yoshiwara* (reed-moor) of modern times. Thus the reputation of the new enterprise sank still lower, and by and by the conduct of the *danseuses*— whose number had now grown to nearly a hundred and fifty—being deemed injurious to public morals, the law stepped in and interdicted their performance. This happened in the year 1643. It

was an event of great moment to the develop- ment of the histrionic art in Japan, for from that time actresses were never permitted to perform in company with actors, and it be- came necessary that the female *rôles* should be taken by men. Apparently such a veto should have proved a serious obstacle, but in truth its effect was small.

From the days of Genzaemon, a skilled musician and dancer who went from Kyoto to Yedo in the middle of the seven- teenth century, carrying with him a ward- robe of female finery and astounding his contemporaries by his perfect studies of feminine ways, the playing of women's parts by men has been carried to an extraordinary degree of excellence. It happens again and again that the deception is so perfect as to defy the closest scrutiny. Even to those fully cognizant that mixed acting has not yet been introduced, it is sometimes impossible to believe that an innovation of that kind has not been effected. All the indescribable

A "NO" DANCER IN COSTUME.

graces and subtle refinements of feminine deportment are reproduced with absolute fidelity, and it becomes easy to credit an assertion often made by persons familiar with the "green room," that such results are obtained only by acting the woman till the simulation becomes unconscious, and is preserved as faithfully in every-day life as on the stage.[1] We may add here that although the old interdict no longer holds, the exclusive custom still prevails. Actresses there are,—two or three companies,—but their moral reputation is of the worst, and it is thought that their admission to the stage proper would sink it again to the low level from which it has barely begun to rise. Thus the *onna-shibai* (women's theatre) remains a thing apart, and until a new generation of *artistes* are specially educated, the ban of ostracism

---

[1] There is a well-known and fairly well attested story that, on the occasion of a conflagration at a theatre, one of these male actresses thought only of saving his hand mirror. That they are constantly courted by amorous rustics unacquainted with theatrical usages is certain.

will continue in force. But these comments depart from the sequence of our history. It is a confused history, if we follow Japanese records; a history in which the growth of the drama itself has no concern for the narrator in comparison with the biographies of individual performers and the vicissitudes of their enterprise. By the middle of the seventeenth century, we find a term[1] employed which indicates that the histrionic element of the dance had assumed prominence, but it may be broadly stated that until the early years of the eighteenth century theatrical performances were only a special variety of the mimes already described under the name of *no-kyogen* and popularized as *kabuki*. The dancers, by gesture and facial expression, portrayed the motives and sentiments attributed to them by a chorus of singers, but remained always mute themselves. Marionette shows had much to do with the development of the true drama. Their use in association with music and song dated from about the year 1605, and gradually attained such a degree of elaboration that the task of composing puppet plays began to occupy the attention of men of letters. Early in the eighteenth century, two dramatists, Chikamatsu Monzaemon and Takeda Izumo, adapted for the marionette stage celebrated historical incidents, like the vendetta of the Forty-seven *Ronin*, and the expulsion of the Dutch from Formosa by the pirate King Kokusen-ya (known in European annals as Coxinga). These men were the fathers of the Japanese drama, and it is a noteworthy fact that their talent as playwrights was without precedent in its time and has remained without peer ever since. The magnificent costumes of the marionettes were adopted by the actors; wigs took the place of the kerchiefs previously wrapped round the head; scenery was added, and at last the drama reached its present stage of development.

This skeleton record has a value not merely historical. It brings into prominence the two factors that have chiefly operated in the development of the Japanese drama, namely, that the performances took place originally in the open air and that they had a choragic accompaniment. A necessary result of the former was that the dais where the acting had its focus did not constitute the limits of the stage. Instead of emerging from mysterious regions behind doors or partitions, the performers throughout the whole course of their comings and goings remained under the eyes of the audience. The very rudiments of art prescribed such a method in the case of dancing; for motion to be perfectly musical must be smooth and continuous, the dancer must enter the field of vision without any violent transition from rest to activity. Hence it was quickly understood that he must dance to the dais, and out of that canon grew the idea of making a route from the back of the auditorium to the stage. It was appropriately bounded by lines of blossoms, and thus received the name "flower path" (*hana-michi*). Another result of the *alfresco* performance was that the environment of the stage had to be included in the scenic *ensemble*. The stage became merely a part of a general scheme of decoration in which not only the auditorium but also

[1] *Mono-mane kyogen*, which literally signifies "imitative *divertissement*." *Kyogen*, in its original sense, means farcical or burlesque, language, but was used with reference to the entertainment furnished by the choric monologues rather than to any extravagance in their diction.

A FUNERAL PROCESSION.

The Japanese show great respect for the dead, and the ceremonial both at the house and grave is very impressive. Until recently all funerals, even those of Shinto priests, were conducted by Buddhist priests, but now the Shintoists are permitted to bury their own believers. White is the Shinto color of mourning, but according to the Buddhist ritual the pall-bearers are clad in dark blue. Shaven priests carrying curious representations of the lotus flower in white and gold attend the bier. Mourners carry banners from the Shinto temples, and large clusters of artificial flowers. The Shinto coffin is a square box, in which the remains are placed in a sitting posture with the head bent to the knees; it is suspended from long poles and carried like a sedan chair. The family of the deceased follow in kagos or jinrikishas, and a large concourse of friends on foot accompanies them to the grave and returns with them to their residence, where sweetmeats and saké are served for refreshment.

will continue in force. But these comments depart from the sequence of our history. It is a confused history, if we follow Japanese records; a history in which the growth of the drama itself has no concern for the narrator in comparison with the biographies of individual performers and the vicissitudes of their enterprise. By the middle of the seventeenth century, we find a term[1] employed which indicates that the histrionic element of the dance had assumed prominence, but it may be broadly stated that until the early years of the eighteenth century theatrical performances were only a special variety of the mimes already described under the name of *no-kyogen* and popularized as *kabuki*. The dancers, by gesture and facial expression, portrayed the motives and sentiments attributed to them by a chorus of singers, but remained always mute themselves. Marionette shows had much to do with the development of the true drama. Their use in association with music and song dated from about the year 1605, and gradually attained such a degree of elaboration that the task of composing puppet plays began to occupy the attention of men of letters. Early in the eighteenth century, two dramatists, Chikamatsu Monzaemon and Takeda Izumo, adapted for the marionette stage celebrated historical incidents, like the vendetta of the Forty-seven *Ronin*, and the expulsion of the Dutch from Formosa by the pirate King Kokusen-ya (known in European annals as Coxinga). These men were the fathers of the Japanese drama, and it is a noteworthy fact that their talent as playwrights was without precedent in its time and has remained without peer ever since. The magnificent costumes of the marionettes were adopted by the actors; wigs took the place of the kerchiefs previously wrapped round the head; scenery was added, and at last the drama reached its present stage of development.

This skeleton record has a value not merely historical. It brings into prominence the two factors that have chiefly operated in the development of the Japanese drama, namely, that the performances took place originally in the open air and that they had a choragic accompaniment. A necessary result of the former was that the dais where the acting had its focus did not constitute the limits of the stage. Instead of emerging from mysterious regions behind doors or partitions, the performers throughout the whole course of their comings and goings remained under the eyes of the audience. The very rudiments of art prescribed such a method in the case of dancing; for motion to be perfectly musical must be smooth and continuous, the dancer must enter the field of vision without any violent transition from rest to activity. Hence it was quickly understood that he must dance to the dais, and out of that canon grew the idea of making a route from the back of the auditorium to the stage. It was appropriately bounded by lines of blossoms, and thus received the name " flower path " (*hana-michi*). Another result of the *al-fresco* performance was that the environment of the stage had to be included in the scenic *ensemble*. The stage became merely a part of a general scheme of decoration in which not only the auditorium but also

---

[1] *Mono-mane kyogen*, which literally signifies " imitative *divertissement*." *Kyogen*, in its original sense, means farcical, or burlesque, language, but was used with reference to the entertainment furnished by the choric monologues rather than to any extravagance in their diction.

A FUNERAL PROCESSION.

The Japanese show great respect for the dead, and the ceremonial both at the house and grave is very impressive. Until recently all funerals, even those of Shinto priests, were conducted by Buddhist priests, but now the Shintoists are permitted to bury their own believers. White is the Shinto color of mourning, but according to the Buddhist ritual the pall-bearers are clad in dark blue. Shaven priests carrying curious representations of the lotus flower in white and gold attend the bier. Mourners carry banners from the Shinto temples, and large clusters of artificial flowers. The Shinto coffin is a square box, in which the remains are placed in a sitting posture with the head bent to the knees; it is suspended from long poles and carried like a sedan chair. The family of the deceased follow in kagos or jinrikishas, and a large concourse of friends on foot accompanies them to the grave and returns with them to their residence, where sweetmeats and saké are served for refreshment.

the whole space within the range of the spectator's vision were comprised. At first the dancers set up a dais wherever space was conveniently available; no special steps were taken to provide accommodation for the audience. But by and by a semicircular platform was erected for the better classes of spectators. This innovation is perpetuated in the nomenclature of the theatre, for inasmuch as "deadheads" made a habit of peeping at the performance through the scaffolding that supported the platform, they received the name of *uzura* (quails) in allusion to their stooping posture, and by that name the portion of the auditorium immediately below the gallery continues to be called to-day.

From the erection of this crescent of seats to the complete enclosure of the place of performance and the building of a permanent hall, progress was natural and quick. The theatre assumed a form which has varied little during the past century. There is a pit divided into a number of little cubicals with matted floors where the people sit, *more Japonico;* there are tiers of boxes on either side; there is a broad corridor at the back, and to the right and left of the stage there are elevated boxes for the chorus and the reciters, who are almost concealed from the audience by bamboo blinds. All these arrangements are simple and somewhat rude; the comfort of the spectator is little consulted. The stage revolves. How and when that excellent idea occurred to the Japanese, we have no evidence. They did not get it from China or India, and it can scarcely have come to them through

ancient Grecian traditions. The element of naturalness and realism that it adds to the performance cannot be overestimated. It doubles the scope of the representation. The outside of a house is shown, and so is everything that passes outside by way of preliminary to what is about to occur within. Then the stage revolves and the same actors appear in the indoor scene. Elaborations of such a facility are innumerable and will be easily conceived without any detailed description.

STREET SCENE IN YOKOHAMA.

The "flower road" is an important adjunct. An underground passage enables the actor to get from the back of the stage to a point behind the auditorium, whence he emerges on the *hana-michi* and makes his way through the audience to the stage. He is acting all the while, perhaps conferring with a companion as to the course to be pursued when they reach their destination, perhaps stealing along to effect a surprise, perhaps hesitating about the welcome that awaits him, perhaps lingering in the reluctance of a final farewell. The effect is not merely to enhance the realism and deepen the interest, but also to make the whole audience participate in the action of the drama and to enable accessory incidents to be developed simultaneously with the unfolding of the central plot. A similar extension of dramatic capabilities results from the choragic adjunct. On the stage of the Occident dialogue, monologue or a "situation " is always necessary. That vast domain of every-day life where the lips are silent, though the mental preludes or consequences of important events are in full progress, cannot be shown without violating truth. The performer is obliged to think aloud even though breathless silence be prescribed by all the probabilities of the scene. He has to interrupt the action of the plot in order to take the audience into his confidence, in order to unveil sentiments which did they really control his acts would never tolerate such interruptions. The Japanese method does not compel speech to play that exaggerated and unnatural part in the drama of life. Monologues are not sanctioned unless the situation is such as to evoke them naturally. Sometimes a great part of a scene takes place without any interchange of words or any use of speech by the actors. They confine themselves to depicting moods or performing acts which the choragic reciter explains. The pantomime is admirable, occasionally a little exaggerated, but reaching on the whole to an extraordinarily high standard of mimetic art. That is the natural result of a system which assigns as much importance to the mimetic side of the drama as to the spoken. It is probably safe to affirm that the Japanese are the greatest mimics in the world.

There is, however, one feature which contrasts strangely with this obedience to the verities. The mechanics of the drama are suffered to obtrude themselves upon public observation through the medium of stage attendants. These persons, draped and veiled in "invisible" colors, are appropriately called "blacks" (*kurombo*). They openly assist at the intricate transformations of costume occasionally demanded by the progress of the play, and they clear the stage of encumbrances which, in an Occidental theatre, would necessitate a tableau and fall of the curtain. Thus a veiled figure may be seen, now aiding a dancer to emerge, chrysalis-like, from a sombre surcoat into a butterfly robe; now holding a little curtain of black cloth between the audience and a supposed corpse while the latter removes itself. Such discordant notes destroy the realistic harmony of the general action. They are, as will readily be conjectured, defects that have descended from the days of marionettes, and within the past few years they have almost disappeared.

In speaking of the Japanese drama a very notable point has to be recorded: the same plays have held the stage for more than a century. We should have a parallel in the West if English theatres had confined themselves to Shakespeare ever since the publication of his works. The Japanese generally knows beforehand exactly what he is to see at the theatre, and knows that his father and his grandfather saw the same piece. New dramatists are now beginning to make their appearance, but the old may be said to occupy the field still. Thus the value that attaches to the skill of the actors cannot be overestimated. There are farces,

of course, — "gossip plays" (*sewa kyogen*), as they are called, — but they serve chiefly to relieve the tension of the drama, and are usually played between the acts of the latter. It must be confessed that until modern times Japanese comedy was distinctly broad. It sometimes employed materials that are banished from the daylight of Western decorum, and derived

VILLAGE STREAM IN MIDSUMMER.

inspiration from incidents that would shock fastidious delicacy in Europe. But these blemishes were usually softened by an atmosphere of naturalness and simplicity. They did not indicate moral debasement such as would accompany similar absence of reserve in a Western country. To interpret them in that manner would have been to mistake artlessness for obscenity. As reasonably might one confound the undisguised diction of the Pentateuch with the prurient coarseness of "Love in a Wood" or "The Country Wife." If Japanese comedy had much in common with the works of Juvenal and Aristophanes, it seldom recalled Wycherley or Congreve. If it sometimes raised a laugh at the grosser phases of life, it scarcely ever became a vehicle for presenting to public imagination the immoral in company with the attractive. And the new civilization may be said to have purged it of all evil elements. In modern Japan a year's advance represents in many cases a decade of progress. The present generation of Japanese are probably as far removed from the license of *pre-Meiji* days as the English of our era are from the indecencies of "The Rake's Progress" and "Tristram Shandy."

The social status of the actor has not yet been appreciably raised. The theatre, indeed, is no longer avoided by the upper classes, but only as a point of special complaisance do they occasionally admit the stars of the stage to their company. In no small degree the actor himself is responsible for this anomaly. With little hope of improving his station he pays little heed to the obligations of respectability. He apparently thinks that a vicious life cannot add much to the disabilities under which he already labors. At the same time fate, with its usual waywardness, impels the professional *danseuse* (*geisha*) to seek in the actor's unconventional society solace for the orderly services that she is obliged to render in aristocratic circles whence the actor is ostracized. With these "butterflies of the banquet" the object of making money is generally to spend it on an actor. One can easily guess how it fares with the actor in the absence of social restraint and in the presence of such strong temptation. Besides, he has not even the solace of knowing that worldly prosperity will reward his talents.

It has always been and still is the rule that a play should run for at least twenty-three days. Very often, of course, the period is extended. For such a term the emoluments of Ichikawa Danjuro, incomparably the greatest actor of his era, are twenty-five hundred *yen*. If, however, he has played in an exceptionally arduous *rôle*, an additional honorarium of from two to three thousand *yen* is given. There are some seven performances yearly. Thus Danjuro's annual income is from ten to fifteen thousand gold dollars. Out of that total, however, he has to disburse large sums for the hire of his costumes, which are not provided by the theatre, and for the support of pupils (*deshi*) who constitute a kind of society to promote his influence and perpetuate his style. Moreover, the unwritten law of the actor's profession requires that he shall live on a scale of lavish expenditure. Apart from the tendency, encouraged by his art, to court public notice by magnificent ostentation, there is an instinctive resort to that agreeable method of self-advertisement, and there is also an unconfessed but powerful desire to prove that fortune favors him though aristocrats are unkind. Thus the comings and goings of great actors partake of the nature of royal progresses. They never descend to the *rôle* of a humble citizen. Everywhere they carry the stage with them, and whether they visit a spa in the dog days, or take an evening's outing on a river, or organize a picnic to view "snow flowers," or go on a fishing expedition, or stay at home, they are always acting the *grand seigneur* in fact as well as in fashion. The inimitable Danjuro, indeed, departs somewhat from these extravagances, and it is just to add that he is a conspicuous exception to the common rule of licentious living. But, on the whole, the actor and his art alike suffer from abuses which are, perhaps, the inevitable outgrowth of an unhonored employment. The lessee of a theatre is at the mercy of a capitalist; the actor at that of the property man. The lessee generally has no capital but his official license; the capitalist has a list of the theatre's liabilities, contracted some in the present, some in the past, and usually aggregating a sum beyond all reasonable possibility of liquidation. The bulk of the theatrical wardrobe is owned by merciless monopolists who extort the last *sen* for the use of a costume. From the capitalist the lessee receives at each representation just enough money to defray current expenses, and for that accommodation is required not merely to repay the advance, but also to set aside from the takings interest at the rate of thirty or forty per cent.

Thus actor and lessee alike are weighted by a heavy load of debt. That theatrical enterprise should show little vitality under such circumstances is natural. An attempt has indeed been made to improve the stage, the scenery and the equipment of the house, but the results have not been so successful as to warrant the extension of the effort beyond one theatre. The low status of the profession is still glaringly displayed in meagre scenery, rough wooden buildings and accommodations of the crudest and most comfortless description. Only at the one theatre just spoken of, the *Shintomi-za* or "New-wealth theatre," has the custom of holding representations that last from morning till evening been cut down by a moiety. The waste of time thus entailed and the unwholesome effects of sitting for so many hours in a crowded, ill-ventilated building are not the only evil features of the habit. People who spend the day looking at a play must be provided with meals, and out of that necessity there springs up

HARUNA LAKE, ABOVE IKAO.
The famous temples are several miles below the lake. The bowl of the lake is an extinct crater.

around the theatre a little city of restaurants and tea-houses, all adding to the costliness of the entertainment and subtracting from the productive capacity of the nation. The theatre, in fact, has not shared the general progress of modern Japan. Yet it certainly has a great future before it, for, in addition to the unique features of which we have spoken, there is histrionic capacity of the very highest order. Ichikawa Danjuro and Onoye Kikugoro, the princes of the stage at present, would long ago have earned a world-wide reputation had their lot been cast in any Western country. There cannot be any second opinion about their capacities, or about their title to rank with the greatest tragedians in the world. But in their own country, though their names are household words, the taint of their profession clings to them still. Men speak of them as a ballet dancer of extraordinary agility or a banjo player of eminent skill would be spoken of in Europe or America — renowned exponents of a renownless art.

From pastimes common to all seasons we turn, for a moment, to the observances of the twelfth month, the "last child" (*otogo*) of the year. Its opening day brings once more upon the scene the perennial rice dumpling, now eaten by all that go down to the sea in ships, a charm against perils of wave and flood. The part played by this particular comestible in Japanese religious rites and ceremonies doubtless excites the reader's curiosity. It is the sacred bread of the nation, but it owes its exalted character to nothing more mysterious than its circular shape, a type of the mirror used to entice the wayward sun goddess from her cave in the days of the beginning of all things. In the cities these quaint customs are gradually fading from public sight, but some of them are preserved from oblivion by the motives that they furnish to artists. Probably no collection of Japanese objects of virtu is without three or four representations in wood, ivory or bronze, of the *tsuina*, or demon-expelling ceremony. In the artist's hands it takes the form of a devil flying from a shower of beans directed against him by a householder in gala costume. The whole ceremony, as practised by the people, is sufficiently depicted by this brief description. On the last night of the old year, the night that divides (*setsu-bun*) winter from spring, parched beans are scattered about the house, with repeated utterance of the formula "out devils, enter fortune" (*oni soto fuku uchi*). There was a time when this rite was performed in the Imperial Court on an imposing scale. Four bands of twenty youths, each wearing a four-eyed mask, a black surcoat and a red body garment, and each carrying a halberd in the left hand, marched simultaneously from the four gates of the palace, driving the devils before them.

A great plague at the beginning of the eighth century suggested the need of this ceremony, and China furnished the programme, but modern Japan is content to bombard with beans the sprite of ill luck, trusting bacteriologists to exorcise the imps of pestilence. Some of the ancient customs, however, have not changed with the times. Industrious women still make offerings of broken needles at the temple of Awashima on the 8th of the month and still abstain from all sewing on that day. In every home there is still a grand "smut sweeping" (*susu-harai*), sometimes on the 13th, sometimes at the close of the month. " Feasts of year forgetting " (*bonen-kai*) are still organized to dispel regrets for the death of another span of life; and in the shadows of the tutelary deities' temples and shrines night fairs are still held, to which the people throng in vast crowds to buy pines of perennial verdure, lobsters of longevity, ropes of perfumed straw, and all the other decorative adjuncts of the season, as well as battle-boards for little girls and kites for boys. The fairs themselves are festivals, bright landmarks in the lives of the young, revivals of fond memories for the old.

XIII

JAPAN'S COMMERCIAL AND POLITICAL INTERCOURSE
WITH FOREIGN COUNTRIES.

E have now to consider a subject which has already engaged the pens of many writers, elicited singularly divergent expressions of opinion and provoked extensive controversy the subject of Japan's political and commercial relations with the outer world. It is a subject of much interest, but in order to equip ourselves for its intelligent consideration we must undertake a prefatory inquiry, brief, indeed, but deterrent to the general reader. We must learn something about the media of exchange in old Japan; something about the ratio between the precious metals and the manner of their circulation; something about the remuneration of labor and the prices of staple commodities; and something about the attitude of officialdom toward trade. These things occupy a more or less important place in every chapter of the story.

In Japan, as in Europe, old-time officialdom regarded the realm of trade as falling within its legitimate control. From time to time edicts were issued fixing the prices of commodities and prescribing the method of conducting transactions. As early as the beginning of the eighth century a ministry of finance was organized, and the name then given to it remains in use to this day. Its functions extended not merely to matters of finance, but also to determining the exchangeable values of coins and goods, and further to regulating weights and measures. This reference to coins indicates that they existed in Japan at an early epoch. The courageous chroniclers of the semi-mythical Empress Jingo (201 A. D.) allege that among the spoils carried by her from Korea were coins in the shape of a bird, but those curiosities remain a mere tradition. Not until the year 485 A. D. does any trustworthy record present itself. Silver coins seem to have served as tokens of exchange at that era. But they were not in common use. The Japanese did not possess stores of precious metal sufficient for purposes of currency. There were no mines in the country. Whenever gold or silver came across the sea in the form of gifts or tribute from China or Korea, the casting of idols suggested itself as the natural use for these rare and beautiful objects, and if they were not devoted to that pious end, they served as personal ornaments, or were employed in the decorative arts. It must not be inferred that the Japanese, at any era of their history, practised the savage fashion of thrusting circlets of the precious metals through their ears or noses, or loading themselves with collars, rings and bracelets of gold and silver. The insecurity of property to which that barbarous fancy owed its origin was happily unknown in Japan. Gold and silver were esteemed chiefly for their beauty. They entered into costume in the form of embroidery. They were used for embellishing weapons of war and inlaying armor. Considerable quantities were absorbed by the

lacquerer and the sculptor in the shape of dust and leaf, and up to the middle of the seventh century it was customary to place in the coffin of a deceased aristocrat, portions not only of the noble metals, but also of copper and iron. Not until 675 A. D. was silver discovered within the Japanese realm. The island of Tsushima furnished it, and of the first supply forwarded to the government, portions were offered to the gods, --which means, of course, that they came into the possession of the priests, --the rest being distributed among officials and men of rank. The discovery of copper followed that of silver by twenty-three years, and at the close of the seventh century a mint was established where, according to the records, coins of gold, silver, copper and iron were struck, though it must be noted that neither the silver nor the gold tokens were made from metal produced in Japan. From a practical point of view we may consider that the first coinage operations took place during the *Wado* era (708 A. D.) and that the tokens then struck were almost entirely of copper. A silver piece was, indeed, issued, but the quantity was too limited to affect general transactions of trade. Interesting and suggestive measures were adopted by the authorities to put an end to the method of barter hitherto in vogue and to induce the people to accept the new coins as media of exchange - measures evidently dictated by economical principles of Chinese origin. One Imperial edict urged farmers and merchants to appraise their products and commodities in terms of the new tokens, and promised that steps of official rank should be given to persons who accumulated stores of copper *cash;* a second made the possession of a fortune of six thousand *cash* an essential preliminary to promotion in office; a third directed that land sales effected by process of barter, and not by transfer of coin, would involve confiscation of the land; a fourth ordered travellers to carry a stock of coin instead of a store of goods for defraying the expenses of their journey; and a fifth enacted that taxes might be received in coin instead of in kind. Such primeval legislation throws a curious light on the fiscal intelligence of the era. It was quickly followed by the consequences that might naturally have been expected. Scarcely ninety years had elapsed before the government found it necessary to prohibit the hoarding of *cash* and to remind the agricultural class that, in the event of a bad harvest, coins could not be cooked and eaten. But the propensity to hoard had already become epidemic. Another decree quickly followed, declaring that any person who concealed coins and paid his taxes in kind would have his store of cash confiscated, one fifth of the amount being promised to an informer. All through the history of those early centuries we can trace the arbitrariness and the embarrassments of Japan's empirical financiers. The people, of frugal habits and generally in humble circumstances, had little use for exchange media of large denominations. They did not want gold or silver coins, except to a very limited extent, and could not have procured them, for the mintage of such tokens was insignificant. When a merchant came into possession of either gold or silver he paid it out by weight, cutting it into parallelograms of the required size; and in later times—from the eleventh to the sixteenth century—all coinage operations being interrupted by domestic troubles, the precious metals were exported to China to purchase copper tokens, for which alone any really wide use existed. While the mint worked, it turned out from five and one half to one and three quarters millions of copper *cash* annually, figures whose difference furnishes incidental evidence, not merely, as might naturally be supposed, of the variable output of the mines, but also of the prime importance attached in those eras to the worship of heaven. For the chief demand for copper being in connection with the casting of idols, it

BRONZE GATE AND TOMB, SHIBA PARK, TOKYO.

resulted that the quantity available for coinage purposes depended largely upon the fervor of the court's piety, or the need of invoking heaven's aid in some national crisis. Religious zeal thus became responsible for the earliest debasement of the coinage. During the first hundred years of minting operations, the weight of the copper unit varied within comparatively narrow limits in five issues. But the business of erecting temples and peopling them with images of the gods attained such extraordinary dimensions during the Nara epoch and the opening years of the Heian era that the government, finding the supply of copper inadequate and the treasury exhausted, hit upon the device of debasing the coinage, and the weight of copper in the unit suddenly fell by nearly fifty per cent. Another scheme was to strike special coins to which arbitrary values were given far in excess of their intrinsic values as compared with the unit. The perplexity and confusion resulting from these financial vagaries were of course very great. Even apart from such technical irregularities, it is difficult to imagine how a people of whose refined and almost luxurious habits so much has been written should have resigned themselves to copper monometallism, and conducted nearly all their transactions of exchange with media of which the highest denomination did not exceed a quarter of a cent. Purses there were none of course, at least none to which the term would now be applicable. Money bags were used and boxes, but a hand-cart was the usual means of transporting these *cash*, which were strung on ropes of straw with knots dividing them into hundreds and thousands. It will readily be conceived that the coins themselves were not high specimens of minting technique. The ideographs entering into their superscriptions had generally the honor of being moulded after a copy traced by some renowned or princely caligraphist, but the mint's appliances were rude, and from time to time merchants exercised their judgments so far as to reject defaced coins or accept them at greatly reduced values, discrimination which the Emperor Saga (820 A. D.) checked by flogging the fastidious trader, his Majesty's theory being that the tenderer of a coin was not responsible for its condition or quality and should not be exposed to the risk of a reduced dinner or a curtailed coat because the disk of the token happened to be serrated or its superscription illegible.

It cannot be doubted that in the government's defective and dishonest coinage is to be found one of the causes which contributed to blunt what philosophers have called "the commercial conscience" in Japan. In the realm where strict integrity was conspicuously

FUNERAL SERVICE IN A SHINTO TEMPLE.

essential to the safe conduct of tradal affairs, an example of selfish unscrupulousness was set by those to whom the people were naturally entitled to look for standards of morality. Comparing the Chinese and the Japanese, there is a consensus of foreign opinion that the former have the keener appreciation of the value of honesty as a commercial policy. That view derives support from the events of which we are writing. The copper coins obtained by Japan from her neighbor were always intrinsically more trustworthy than those struck by herself, and the people showed their appreciation of the fact by circulating the former at four times the exchange value of the latter. Strenuous efforts were made by the government to prevent such discrimination. It seems to have been regarded as a species of *lèse-majesté* that a farmer or a trader, a "common fellow," should venture to prefer a foreign coin to a domestic, or, in the matter of Japanese tokens, should exercise a right of choice between

pieces which, whatever their variations of intrinsic value, were uniformly franked by sovereign sanction. Need it be recorded that the victory ultimately rested with the people? A good many were scarred in the fight, carried to their graves stigmata branded on their cheeks by official irons; others paid the penalty of three days' exposure on the public highway, and had the chagrin of seeing every member of their village fined for their sin of "shroffing." But in Tokugawa days the government abandoned the fight, and the Chinese cash were definitely recognized as possessing four times the value of their Japanese contemporaries.

Brought now to the question of the purchasing power of these liliputian coins, we are prepared to find that it bore a very high ratio to their intrinsic value, in accordance with the venerable rule that the smaller the denomination of the unit of exchange, the greater its relative value in terms of commodities. The standard measure of capacity

METHOD OF DRESSING THE HAIR (FOR MEN)
BEFORE THE REVOLUTION OF 1867.

in Japan is a *koku* (5.13 bushels), which is decimally subdivided into *to, sho* and *go*. Many notices of the price officially fixed for rice are found in the old chronicles. Almost without exception it was one *cash (mon)* per *go*, or a thousand *cash* per *koku*. This very convenient assessment at once suggests an important fact; namely, that rice itself was a standard of

value. That has been the case down to the latest times. Taxes, as we have seen, were originally levied in the form of a percentage of the gross produce of a farm. Then, when copper
having been discovered here and there throughout the empire, supplies of it became desirable
for minting purposes, the government enacted, first, that taxes might be paid in that metal,
and, subsequently, that they should be paid in coin; changes obviously necessitating an official
assessment of the *koku* in terms of *cash*. Fiscal convenience dictated the simplest possible
assessment, so the *koku* was declared to represent one *kwan* (1,000 *cash*), and its thousandth
subdivision, the *go*, became the equivalent of one *cash*. Of course nature, notably capricious
in sub-tropical countries like Japan, did not lend constant sanction to such an arbitrarily fixed
value. Sometimes a *koku* of rice sold in the open market for nearly twice the official figure,
and once, in time of famine (867 A. D.), it rose to eight times that figure. But even as late
as the era of the " Shadow Shoguns " of Kamakura (1230) the government, maintaining its
theoretical independence of storms and inundations, clung to the old assessment of one *go*
for one *mon*, and we may assert, without much risk of error, that up to comparatively modern
times the official figure corresponded with the true market measure. A laborer in Japan is
credited with capacity to consume 5 *go* (1½ pints) of rice daily ; a man of refined habits is
allowed 3 *go*. It is thus seen that in old times a thousand *cash* purchased from 200 to 333
days' supply of rice for an adult. The same quantity now costs fourteen times as much.

Rice is a great deal more to the Japanese than bread is to an Occidental people, and
a little less than bread and meat in combination. Even in this era of railroads and steam-
boats there are many Japanese to whom a cup of rice is as great a treat, and as rare, as a
beefsteak to an Irish squatter. In the early and middle ages, not a few unblessed rustics
lived and died without knowing the taste of the precious grain. Barley, millet, pickled tur-
nip, or some other vegetable, a modicum of salted fish or seaweed, and a seasoning of soy,
such was the farmer's fare. Rough as it was he invested its consumption with an air of
ceremony and punctilio. Unlike the Chinaman, whose bowl of condiments is common to
the chop-sticks of all the convives, each Japanese had his own special utensils and his own
particular tray to support them. A lacquered bowl containing soup made by boiling shreds
of dried bonito with soy and garden stuff ; a tiny plate of pungent *daikon* and salted egg-
plant; a saucer of pickled greens, — with such luxuries was the feast spread. But everything
occupied the rank of a mere relish compared with the *pièce de résistance*, rice; supposing that
article of diet to be within the feaster's means. The difference was vividly illustrated in
the manner of using the chop-sticks. They played the part of dainty triflers on their visits
to the bowls and plates, picking up a morsel here or a shred there; but when they had to do
with the rice, they were suddenly converted into vigorous shovels for packing the mouth with
substantial portions from the soft white pile.